MY FIRST BOOK OF BABY SIGNS

BABY

BED

CAR

EAT

BATH

MORE

UP

SHOES

MILK

HAT

MY FIRST BOOK OF
BABY SIGNS

40 ESSENTIAL SIGNS TO LEARN AND PRACTICE

LANE REBELO

ILLUSTRATIONS BY CAIT BRENNAN

CALLISTO
PUBLISHING

My sweetest memories are of reading bedtime stories to my "babies" when they were still small enough to fit on my lap. I hope this book will become a part of your sweet memories as well.

Copyright © 2021 by Callisto Publishing LLC
Cover and internal design © 2021 by Callisto Publishing LLC
Illustrations © Cait Brennan; © vectorscore/Shutterstock: 42–44 (alphabet); © Chloé Besson: 44 (numbers)
Author photo courtesy of Jacquelyn Warner

Art Director: Karmen Lizzul
Art Producer: Hannah Dickerson
Editor: Laura Apperson

Callisto Publishing and the colophon are registered trademarks of Callisto Publishing LLC.

Published by Callisto Publishing LLC C/O Sourcebooks LLC
P.O. Box 4410, Naperville, Illinois 60567-4410
(630) 961-3900
callistopublishing.com

This product conforms to all applicable CPSC and CPSIA standards.

Source of Production: Wing King Tong Paper Products Co.Ltd. Shenzhen, Guangdong Province, China
Date of Production: September 2023
Run Number: 5034795

Printed and bound in China.
WKT 24

NOTE TO CAREGIVERS

Welcome to *My First Book of Baby Signs*! This book combines two of my favorite things: baby sign language and children's books. Story time is perfect for teaching and practicing American Sign Language (ASL) with your child. *My First Book of Baby Signs* has been designed to encourage your baby to learn new words and signs as you read together.

You can start using this book with your little one as soon as you start reading to them. It's never too early! Most babies will start signing back to you when they are about 8 to 12 months old, though some babies might sign earlier or later. The illustrations of children  modeling the signs are a little older than the babies in the story because older children are able to sign with greater accuracy than babies and young toddlers. Your baby's early attempts at signing can look quite different from how you model it, and that's perfectly fine! Like early spoken words, your baby's early signs will be a rough approximation of what you model.

When you come to the ASL word in the story, sign it as you read. There are descriptions and illustrations on the pages to show you how to make each sign correctly. If your little one signs back, resist the temptation to correct their early signs. Just continue modeling the sign correctly and in time, as their skills develop, their signing will become more accurate. And remember to keep an eye out for repetitive and purposeful hand movements. If you see your baby moving their hands in a new way, there's a good chance they're trying to sign to you! Check out the back of the book for an ASL alphabet chart and examples of the handshapes mentioned in the sign descriptions. You can also find a video dictionary for all the signs in this story at TinySigns.com/book-owner.

Happy signing!

Good morning! Baby is awake and wants to be picked up.

Extend your pointer finger and move it upward.

MOMMY

Mommy says, "Good morning!" and gives Baby a kiss.
Good morning, Mommy!

With an open hand,
tap your thumb on
your chin a few times.

DADDY

Where is Daddy? Peekaboo! There he is!

With an open hand, tap your thumb on your forehead a few times.

MILK

The Babies are drinking milk from bottles. Yummy!

Open and close your hand a few times, like you're milking a cow.

MORE

Baby's milk is all gone, but he's still hungry. Baby wants more!

Touch your fingertips to your thumbs on both hands. Then, tap your fingertips together a few times.

HOT

Baby's cereal is hot. Mommy blows on it. Now it's just right!

Start with one curved hand in front of your mouth, then quickly turn it away like you're removing something hot.

EAT

Yum, yum! Baby can eat all by himself. Good job!

Touch your fingertips to your thumb on one hand. Then, tap your fingertips to your lips a few times, like you are putting food in your mouth.

BANANA

Baby loves bananas! Mommy peels the banana for Baby.

Keeping your index finger and thumb together, move from the top of your opposite index finger downward, like you are peeling a banana. Repeat this motion a second time.

DRINK

Baby is thirsty. He takes a drink from his cup. That's better!

Tip an imaginary cup at your mouth with one hand, like you are taking a drink.

CAT

Meow! Baby wants to pet the cat. Be gentle, Baby.

Pretend to pinch your cheek with your thumb and index finger. Then pull your hand outward as if to show a cat's whiskers.

DOG

Woof, woof! The dog wants to play! Does Baby want to play, too?

Use one hand to pat the side of your thigh, like you are calling a dog to come to you.

PLAY

Baby loves to play! What toy should Baby play with next?

Make a Y handshape with both hands and twist your wrists a few times.

BEAR

Look at Baby's bear. It's so big and soft!

Cross your arms and bend your fingers like bear claws. Then, scratch your shoulders.

SHOES

What did Baby find? Those are Daddy's shoes. Silly Baby!

Make two fists and knock them together, like you're knocking dirt off your shoes.

HAT

Baby is wearing Mommy's hat. Does it fit? No, it's too big!

Pat the top of your head with a flat hand to show where your hat goes.

READY

It's time to go, Baby. Are you ready? Let's go to the park!

Make the R handshape with both hands and shake them slightly from side to side.

CAR

Vroom, vroom! Daddy takes Baby for a ride in the car.

Position your fists as if holding a steering wheel. Move them up and down like you're driving.

HAPPY

Who is happy to be at the park? Baby is!

Brush one flat hand up your chest a few times, like you're showing the happiness in your heart!

FRIEND

Baby is excited to see his friend. Let's play together, friend!

Make the X handshape with both index fingers. Hook them together, then switch them.

BALL

Daddy tosses the ball to Baby. Catch the ball, Baby!

Curve your fingers on both hands like you're holding a ball and bring them toward each other twice.

BABY

Baby is playing with her baby doll. She has a baby of her own!

Cradle your arms in front of your chest. Swing them gently, like you are rocking a baby.

PLEASE

Baby is hungry for a snack. He says, "Please," to ask for one.

Rub one flat hand in a circular motion on your chest.

CRACKER

Yum, yum! Crackers are Baby's favorite snack.

Make fists with both hands. Then, knock the inside of your fist of your dominant hand twice on the elbow of your opposite arm.

WATER

Now Baby is thirsty. Daddy helps Baby drink some water.

Make the W handshape with one hand and tap it twice to your chin.

ALL DONE

Baby is all done. It's time to help clean up!

Hold your open
hands with palms
facing you and twist
them away from
you twice.

HURT

Uh-oh! Baby fell down. That hurt!

Bring your pointer fingers together in front of you, or in front of the body part that hurts.

HELP

It's okay! Mommy is here to help. Is that better?

Place your dominant hand in a thumbs-up shape on your opposite palm, then lift both hands together slightly.

GRANDMA

It's time to see Grandma. She wants to give Baby a big hug!

Start with the thumb of your open hand touching your chin, then bounce your hand away from your chin twice.

GRANDPA

Grandpa builds a tower with Baby. Look how tall it is!

Start with the thumb of your open hand touching your forehead, then bounce your hand away from your forehead twice.

THANK YOU

Grandma gives Baby a yummy treat. Baby says, "Thank you!"

Place the fingertips of your flat hand on your chin, then move your hand outward.

LOVE

Baby loves her family and they love her.

Cross your arms
over your chest and
squeeze them to you.

CHANGE

Baby's diaper is wet. Daddy changes Baby's diaper so he will be clean and dry.

Stack your closed fists on top of each other with fingers touching. Flip over your hands so the hand on the bottom is now on top.

POTTY

Sometimes, Baby uses the potty. Good job, Baby!

Make a T handshape with one hand. Hold it up and shake it slightly from side to side.

BATH

Splish, splash! It's time for Baby's bath! Baby loves to play in the tub.

Make fists with both hands and gently scrub your chest up and down.

COLD

Brrrrrr! Baby is cold. Daddy wraps him up in a cozy towel.

Hold your arms close to your body with closed fists. Shake them quickly, as if shivering.

BOOK

It's almost bedtime. Daddy reads the Babies their favorite book.

Place your hands flat together, then open them outward, like you are opening a book.

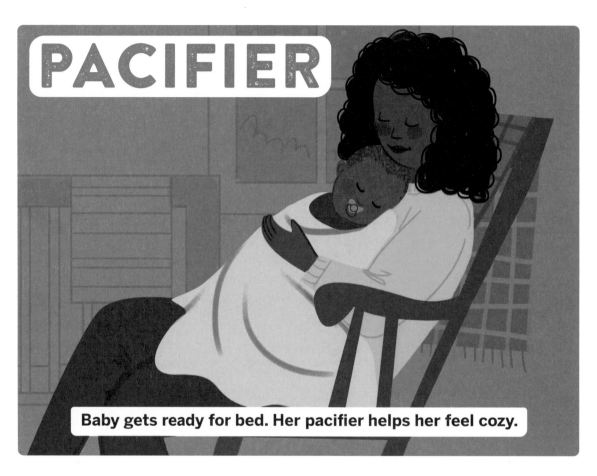

PACIFIER

Baby gets ready for bed. Her pacifier helps her feel cozy.

Make a modified C handshape using only your index finger and thumb. Then, tap your index finger and thumb twice at your mouth.

BED

It's been a fun day. Now Baby is sleepy. Time for bed, Baby!

Tilt your head to the side and rest it on the palm of your flat hand.

LIGHT

Daddy turns off the light. Good night, Baby!

Raise your hand above your head and bring your fingertips together, pointed downward. Open and close your fingers a few times.

I LOVE YOU

Mommy and Daddy each say, "I love you, Baby. Sweet dreams!"

Hold one hand up with your palm facing forward and just your thumb, index finger, and pinkie finger extended.

ALPHABET AND NUMBERS GUIDE

 A Make a fist with palm facing out and thumb pointing up at the side.

 B Make a flat hand with palm facing out, fingers touching, and thumb tucked in.

 C Curve your hand into a *C* shape.

 D Curve all fingers to touch thumb except pointer, which is extended up.

 E Let all fingertips rest along thumb with palm facing out.

 F Bend pointer finger to touch thumb with fingers open, palm facing out.

 G Close hand in a fist with pointer finger and thumb pointing to the side, palm facing in.

 H Close hand in a fist with pointer and middle fingers pointing to the side, palm facing in.

 I Close hand with pinkie finger pointing up and palm facing out.

 J Draw a *J* in the air with pinkie finger.

K Raise pointer and middle fingers up in a *V* shape with thumb tucked into the base of the *V*.

 L Raise pointer finger up and thumb to the side to make an *L* shape with palm facing out.

With palm facing out, fold first three fingers over thumb, which is holding down pinky.

M

 Place first two fingers over thumb, which is holding down pinky and ring finger, with palm facing out.

N

 Touch all fingers to thumb to make an *O* shape.

O

 **Point pointer and middle fingers down in a *V* shape with thumb tucked into the base of the *V*.**

P

 Close hand in a fist with pointer finger and thumb pointing down.

Q

 Twist pointer and middle fingers together with palm facing out.

R

 Close hand in a fist with thumb over closed fingers and palm facing out.

S

 Close hand with thumb tucked between first two fingers and palm facing out.

T

 Point pointer and middle fingers up, touching, with palm facing out.

U

 Point pointer and middle fingers up and spread into a *V* shape with palm facing out.

V

 Point first three fingers up and spread into a *W* shape with palm facing out.

W

Close hand in a fist with pointer finger up and bent, palm facing out.

X

Y Close hand with thumb and pinkie extended, palm facing out.

 Z Draw a *Z* in the air with pointer finger.

 1 Close hand with pointer finger pointing up and palm facing either in or out.

 2 Point pointer and middle fingers up and spread into a *V* shape with palm facing either in or out.

 3 Extend and spread open pointer finger, middle finger, and thumb with palm facing either in or out.

 4 Point all fingers up and spread open with thumb tucked in, palm facing either in or out.

 5 Open hand wide with palm facing either in or out.

 6 Touch pinkie finger to thumb, with remaining fingers spread open and palm facing out.

 7 Touch ring finger to thumb, with remaining fingers spread open and palm facing out.

 8 Touch middle finger to thumb, with remaining fingers spread open and palm facing out.

 9 Touch pointer finger to thumb, with remaining fingers spread open and palm facing out.

 10 Make a thumbs-up gesture with one hand and give it a little shake.

INDEX OF VOCABULARY TERMS

ACKNOWLEDGMENTS

Writing this book felt like writing a love letter to my two children. The illustrations on each and every page are pulled from my own memories of their baby and toddler years. Thank you to Cait Brennan for doing such a beautiful job bringing these illustrations to life.

A heartfelt thank you to Laura Apperson, my editor for this book. I am so grateful to you for your encouragement, support, and patience throughout the process.

Thank you to Callisto Media for the opportunity to create another book. I never dreamed I'd be a published author of one book, much less three. This book is the one I always wanted to create and making it was truly a dream come true.

Of course, thank you to my amazing kids, Clara and AJ, for being so fun, creative, and full of love. I'm so lucky to be your mom. Thanks also to my best friend, André, for your never-ending faith and confidence in me.

Lastly, thank you to the extended Tiny Signs® community. I am so fortunate to have such a kind and vibrant community of dedicated parents and early childhood professionals throughout the US and around the world.

ABOUT THE AUTHOR

 **LANE REBELO, LCSW,** is the author of the best-selling *Baby Sign Language Made Easy: 101 Signs to Start Communication with Your Child Now* and *The Complete Guide to Baby Sign Language: 200+ Signs for You and Baby to Learn Together*. She is the founder of Tiny Signs®, an award-winning baby sign language program. Lane lives with her husband and two children in MetroWest Boston. You can find her online at TinySigns.com.